AF268475

How to Read My Poems

I am an ordinary guy living a middle class life. I may
imagine what it would be like to put on a wingsuit
and jump off a mountain, but my stock-in-trade is the
exploration of "everyday mind." I look for transcendent
meaning in the ordinary happenings of daily life. I write
in the morning everyday, and try to distill experience
down to essentials. It is easy to overlook the instant-by-
instant process of seeing, thinking, and responding to
life — but in reality that is what life is.

The mind is self-interested and driven by powerful emotions. I look around and determine what to do. I judge
what's worthy, and establish a list of priorities. My likes
and dislikes become signposts, and if I am not careful
I find myself repeating a pattern of behavior, and get
stuck, narrowly seeing, feeling, experiencing — and then
where is novelty?

Spring has sprung but today is chilly. I love watching the
seasons change in a succession of little details, because
the seasons are so much bigger than what's going on
in my mind. There is always a lot going on in nature,
and my practice is to open, so that more of reality may
penetrate my consciousness.

I practice opening my awareness to the world inside and
outside of me. Consciousness is a miracle — but I have
to learn how to use the gift of Consciousness. This is
what my poetry is about.

My daughter, Jocelyn MacDonald, is a wonderful artist.
Her art work graces this book.

I am Barry MacDonald. I received the *dharma* name,
Tekkan, which means, Iron Man, a settled practitioner of
great determination.

— *Tekkan*

Everyday Mind XIV

A couple of clouds
drifting southeast
give the morning
a gentle air
of evanescence.

It's joyous to have a year every four
Years that we are calling leap year within
Which there is an extra day inserted
In the calendar on February

29 because people are surprised
And befuddled and if you read as I
Do a daily meditation book you
Discover February 29

Isn't there which is like being given
A gift of day on which the demands
Of time are extinguished and the aging
Process is dissolved so I exult as

If I were a bored and overburdened
Student presented with a holiday.

Our best technology
can't keep pace with
the earth's elliptical
orbit around the
sun.

I groaned with the realization of
An unavoidable dilemma
Impacting so powerfully because
Of my habitual inattention

To detail as I recognized I can't
Take part in the poetry instruction
Offered by Donna who intrigues me and
Also attend the annual meeting

Of my Zen Bridge group at exactly the
Same time and what do I do wanting to
Admire Donna and know her better
While also looking forward to being

With so many of my optimistic
Friends celebrating our togetherness?

I can only put off
deciding for another
day as Saturday is
coming.

My daughter came to request some things from
The house for my ex-wife and she asked for
The family photos making me question
What to do and I decided to let

Them go even as I knew that they are
Poignant memories that can't be relived
With me remembering differently from
Her and from my daughter and my son as

I can only see them with the lens of
Today as if my present view were of
Conclusions and consequences with a
Weight of emotions as no one else could

Look at them and have the feelings that we
Do even as our feelings will differ.

Seeing the family photos
ten years from now
how much and
what would I
remember?

Jason said that Jupiter's massive presence
Orbiting the sun as it does further
From the sun than the earth is serving as
A shield deflecting or absorbing the

Cosmic debris that otherwise would strike
The earth and then Jason talked about a
Phenomenon called the Barycenter
That determines the point around which the

Planets orbit the sun that is not at
The center of the sun but rather at
A point that is the central pivot of
Mass in motion that sounds so overly

Complicated to me as scientists
Answer the questions that I didn't ask.

The way things are
gets increasingly
complex for clever
people who keep on
asking questions.

I look at the moon seeing it change its
Shape and position high and low in the
Night and I believe before people were
Living in cities and filling the night

With fluorescence and neon and before
Our busy days were consumed with details
As we are now checking our calendars
And staring at our cell phones in our hands

Before electronics hypnotized us
I believe the mystical allure of
The moon must have been so much more potent
So much more of a stimulant for the

Peoples of the earth to ponder visions
Of heaven searching for reassurance.

How much more of a
jewel of the night and
the morning and
the afternoon the moon
must have been.

Apart from our reading communities
Where we share our enthusiasm in
Small gypsy-like gatherings and apart
From the marketing strategy and the

Tech savvy endeavor of composing
Books and the eyes-straining hunt for typos
For correction of inarticulate
Grammar or word choice and the swings from pride

To self-loathing that come with managing
Large numbers of my poems I love the
Sanctuary of pushing distractions
Aside for an hour of clarity

In the morning when I can play with words
And discover what in me needs getting out.

The simplest details have
enormous consequence —
once free of distraction
joy emerges.

Half my life is spent within the darkness
Of night without my thinking about it
But I know that there are trillions of stars
Beyond the few that I can see and I

Know that gravity is crushing inward
That nuclear fusion is exploding
Outwards of every star in a balance
Of nature persisting for billions of

Years and that the velocity of light
Proceeding from a star extending in
All directions is the speediest force
Of nature and yet the light takes billions

Of years from distant stars to reach the earth
And perhaps those stars no longer exist.

There are trillions
and trillions of
stars and yet
darkness
predominates.

The words and lines of my sonnets make a
Straight edge along the left margin while the
Right side is unpredictable because
Even though every line will consist of

Ten syllables the syllables vary
In length which leads me to reflect on how
Regimented effort with guidelines goes
Well with the happy exploration of

Possibility inescapably
Relying upon the conventional
Meaning of words and the habitual
Idioms of the culture I want to

Discover whether I can say something
Worthy of seizing a reader's interest.

An empty sky with
only the daylight passing
through upon the earth
is a transitory and
glorious experience.

My everyday mind consists of little
Insights hardly worthy of notice that
I wouldn't be attending to at
All except for my meditation that's

Revealing to me that naturally
My thoughts are like a ball bouncing down a
Mountain stream unhindered by obstacles
Until emotions get entangled with

Situations making scenarios
Causing me to experience the self-
Created dissatisfaction easy
To fall into and so difficult to

Escape until I recall my thoughts are
Like a ball bouncing down a mountain stream.

Naturally thoughts may
be unhindered by
obstacles if I allow
them to come
and go.

Fear of being rejected was hard to
Overcome but on Match.com I read
Hundreds of profiles gazed at photos
Ventured a formula greeting became

Indifferent to the non-responses
Developing persistence opening
Possibilities returning more than
Once meeting women listening learning

Conversing sampling differences
Transcending my inhibitions playing
With words dreaming anticipating
While needing to reschedule appointments

Cindy on Tuesday Ruth on Thursday and
Lori Friday Cookie this afternoon.

Enticing with
poetry
Xia
Keesa
Joan.

Every poem embodies the seeds of
Poems to be written just as every
Day contains the seeds of approaching days
As my attention is naturally

Drawn to the permutations of the sky
As what a revelation comes when a
Sky with daylight drains away to the west
Presenting such looming questions about

The odd experience of living on
A rotating earth orbiting a sun and
Possessing dormant and growing seasons
As today is overcast and chilly

While yesterday was sunny and warmer
Perfect for our walking around the lake.

Walking around Lake
Harriet with Cookie
I discovered a
beautiful woman I'd
like to know better.

Thank you for talking with me today as
We had the time for expressing ourselves
With me talking about my conundrums
Being enthusiastically a poet

A sober alcoholic a Buddhist
And a conservative politically
With each group of my association
Misapprehending every other group

Which complicates how freely I'm able
To express myself even as I try to
Be transparent and welcoming it's the
Political animosity that's

Currently separating everyone
Into groups despising other groups.

Communication
is easiest with
sober alcoholics
and with my
two cats.

I sometimes wonder what would it be like
To go to sleep and never wake up but
In the everyday world I've come to look
For the little changes signaling the

Shifting into another season as
There was a dusting of snow overnight
In the midst of much warmer days with the
Melting of three months of snow from the ground

While the frost is leaving the earth as I
Noticed this morning it's comfy now to
Walk about the floorboards of my home in
Bare feet again but in Minnesota

We are not so easily fooled into
Believing that spring is almost arrived.

The dusting of snow
reminds me a thaw
in March is often
followed by blizzards
in April.

We are particles and waves coming to
Being with chemicals and molecules
Each of us with beating hearts and breathing
Lungs that beat and breathe of themselves without

Any effort of conscious awareness
Just as the sun combusts itself with a
Balance of gravity crushing inward
Nuclear fusion exploding outwards

Radiating life giving energy
And in my isolation I may think
There's so much exertion necessary
There are so many details to control

I can't possibly succeed of myself
Without taking responsibility.

Being responsible
or letting go
is an exquisitely
balanced pivot
point.

There weren't tests available when I was
Feeling lightheaded and I disbelieved
The power of the Coronavirus
And I ventured to the gym lifted the

Heaviest weights and pedaled on the bike
Vigorously for an hour keeping
My distance from people ignoring the
Virus putting faith in my attitude

When breathing became much more difficult
And not moving necessary as the
Asthma of my body can't be denied
No matter how athletic I am so

I became a spectator lying on
My back watching the broadcasting of news.

Minnesota Governor
Walz ordered the
gyms in the state
closed for at least
two weeks.

I am circulating air about
Myself by inhaling and exhaling
Exactly as the people in China
Did where the pandemic virus arose

A month ago while Saturday night was
A tipping point when I discovered it's
Easiest to breathe when lying flat on
My back and not moving while remaining

Calm perusing a series of murder
Investigations on a cable channel
Occupying me semi-consciously
As turning to my side would congest my

Lungs but being perfectly still seemed to
Open the way to continuous breath.

Calm and rest
in the midst of
difficult breathing
opens a narrow
way to tomorrow.

In every nation businesses and schools
Are closing and people are avoiding
Each other being afraid of catching
The virus through our breathing or handling

Tainted items as the news is broadcast
Continuously with the government
Organizing health care infrastructure
Broadcasting assurance and instructions

Projecting an aura of confidence and
Calm urging everyone to minimize
Contact with each other and to shelter
At home until the wave of infection

Has done its worst while our livelihoods are
Interrupted into difficult months.

Infection
ripples into
chaos.

Society is upside down today
With some people working and others not
As the federal and state governments
Are preventing the gatherings of large

Groups of people and are discouraging
The meeting of more than ten people so
Schools and businesses are closed for at least
Two weeks depending on how successful

The containment of the virus will be
But our enforced separation from each
Other reveals how much I'm depending
On you as you're depending on someone

Who's depending on others as each of
Us is connected to everyone else.

We are
tethered
by breath
words
intentions
decisions
behavior.

Television is gluing everyone
Together with announcements informing
The public of the stay-at-home orders
And of the money to be sent from the

National treasury to each needy
American and of the production
Of anti-virus medications while
I am playing with my phone and using

My fingertips and reading articles
Logging in for videoconferences
With friends in sobriety and I am
Whimsically exploring for love by

Holding the phone lightly to my ear and
Listening to the voices of women.

Voices inside my
head expand
horizons lighten
gloom soothing
isolation.

A blustery wind is swaying the bare
Branches as lines of geese are laboring
To stay in formation high amidst the
Yet higher swirling of clouds within which

The sun is making an occasional
Appearance as on the ground the streets are
Empty with only a jogger or a
Person walking a dog ambling along

As people are adhering to advice
Are not mingling in restaurants or cafes
Not doing unnecessary commerce
Are shut in their homes until the proper

Officials determine the spread of the
Virus has been contained and we can breathe.

Fortunate people
can work from home
while others are
without jobs for
who knows how long?

My home is full of a lot of junk from
Twenty years of raising a family
With the kids grown and gone with the ex-wife
Taking her things when she can so I'm left

With toys video games and books and clothes
With the furniture I want rid of with
Closets and drawers full of people's stuff
That I haven't looked at or touched for years

And all of it has been collecting dust
Interspersed with repairs I've neglected
Because I've been busy with exercise
With operating my publication

But now the gym is closed and I'm out of
Excuses for not redoing my home.

The things in my house
gradually amidst the
discord of my family
became an unbearable
weight upon my mind.

March is dripping every minute with the
Snow on the ground slowly disappearing
Into the sodden grass and soil as mist
Is lingering between the trees and homes

While it's difficult to distinguish the
Sky from the mist with the bare branches so
Jumbled wildly and weirdly still within
The absence of a wind or a bird as

The twisting and turning of the branches
And twigs slowly emerging in the gray
Morning light bespeak an aggressive and
Explosive energy latent at the

Moment within the overhanging and
Dominating quiescence of the trees.

Turning
twisting
bare
twigs
portend an
appetite
for sunlight.

The gyms in Minnesota are closed to
Prevent the spreading of the virus which
Imposes a hole in my routine so
For exercise I run up and down the

Stone steps at the southern end of downtown
Stillwater to the top of a limestone
Bluff attracting the fitness freaks from miles
Away whom I encounter and compare

Myself against on my first day running
Briskly ascending descending five times
Achieving satisfaction until the
Morning afterwards when walking was quite

Excruciating reminding me its
Easy to start and hard to keep going.

I try to count the steps
while ascending
but get confused
coming up with
different sums.

Radio television Internet
Communicate the decisions of the
Politicians and medical experts
Determined to impede the virus by

Halting all but essential commerce for
No one knows how long as we are advised
To keep distance between us because we
Don't want to be Italy overwhelmed

With too many patients struggling for
Breath and not enough ventilators to
Rescue everyone as America
Is manufacturing ventilators

Preparing vaccines experimenting
With available and effective drugs.

Doctors and nurses
are exposed
overwhelmed
without equipment
and masks.

Cable airwaves are transmitting sniping
Criticism over the president's
Braggadocio and unwarranted
Optimism as commentators are

Touting opinion polls while arguing
With each other and attempting to be
Cogent but there's only so much noise on
TV that's bearable while this morning

I noticed the birds have resumed singing
Almost all the snow is gone the soil is
Moist the grass though mostly pale is exposed
To an increasingly strengthening sun

And the presence of the trees inspires
An anticipation of budding leaves.

Soon breezes will be
sounding in the leaves
again while I can
awaken to birdsong
through open windows.

The margin on the left of this poem
Is aesthetically pleasing to my eye
Upholding the effusive expression
Of words as words are skipping across the

Page as the margin is a boundary
Serving an organizing principle
Creating for a series of poems
One upon another the spine of a

Book while the words are an attempt to seize
And embody an ephemera of
Insight and emotion hopefully in
A form communicating a zestful

Experience between a writer and
A reader dissolving separation.

An open book
relies upon a spine
as a glue cohering
something of our fleeting
experience together.

Walking up the steep incline of Myrtle
Street I noticed on my north the roughly
Hewn blocks of limestone characteristic
Of Stillwater stacked upon each other

Forming a wall holding the persisting
Pressure of a hill of earth day after
Day perhaps from the decades when the town
Was a frontier refuge for lumberjacks

Taking a holiday from harvesting
White pine and because the size of each block
Is formidably heavy the massive
Undertaking of construction without

Consideration of delicacy
Makes me think of the brawny lumberjacks.

They were savvy
engineers of force sizing
up the necessary weight
of stone blocks balancing
the assertion of the earth.

The prosaic limestone wall on Myrtle
Street is a world away from the lofty
Inca palace of Machu Picchu set
Upon a tropical pinnacle of

The Andes mountains created more than
Six hundred years ago so precisely
Fitting the much more massive blocks of stone
Without mortar and astronomically

Aligned designed not to hold back the earth
But to express a harmony amidst
The clouds and stars with ancient techniques we
Cannot comprehend today but in praise

We can designate the temple of the
Sun and the chamber the three windows.

Stillwater witnessed
the frontier passage of
burgeoning industry —
Machu Picchu evinces
vanished aristocracy.

Everything is flawed from a painful point
Of view whether the trouble is cancer
Financial difficulty persisting
Loneliness bearing the injustice of

False accusation being the target
Of political persecution or
Having the prosaic habit of a
Negative attitude and even if

A person is safe and unaffected
While others are miserable the tinge
Of apprehension is palpable and
I wish life were otherwise but if it's

Any consolation we don't suffer
Alone and get through trouble together.

The self-absorption
of suffering comes and
goes in relation to the
presence of love.

The president extended the guideline
Another thirty days until the end
Of April advising nonessential
Workers to stay-at-home to limit the

Spread of infection as hotels and parks
And stadiums are converted into
Hospitals as General Motors and
Ford are making ventilators as a

Speedy test for the virus is coming
With the estimate of peak infection
In two weeks with 100,000 to
200,000 fatalities while

Politicians bicker thus becoming
A menace to America's morale.

Wash hands often
clean household surfaces
avoid touching the face
about the mouth nose and eyes
interdicting the virus.

We talked about whether aspen trees were
Conscious of people walking in their midst
When Jason remarked as he and I were
Walking in William O'Brien State Park

That aspen trees aren't like other trees as
They aren't separate from each other but
They come from a shared system of roots and
They are all a single organism

And yes perhaps they emanate a kind
Of consciousness different from ours and
Because Jason is an ecologist
Who understands the evolution and

Interconnection of landscape plants and
Animals his words are penetrating.

Ten thousand years ago
this land was covered
by a sheet of ice without
vegetation or habitation
possible.

We were walking amidst a lower stretch
Of a trail that used to be the course of
The St. Croix River with the spring melting
Of snow and the pooling of water when

The air was full with the overlapping
Ticking of chorus frogs that sounded like
Cicadas to me with the chuckling calls
Of wood frogs and with the peep peep peeping

Of a few of the spring peeper frogs as
Jason predicted that they would become
Quiet as we passed by while the frogs were
Invisible to me when suddenly

The air was empty of sound but alive
With intelligent anticipation.

Jason thrives exploring
the fabric of consciousness
discounting the supposed
superiority of
people.

The queen conch is long gone leaving only
A shell behind that I retrieved from the
Recesses of my basement giving it
A dusting revealing the charm of its

Curving inward lip so brightly pink and
Its curving outward lip so glossy white
Which inspired me to do what people
Are supposed to do which is to hold the

Hollowness of the conch seashell to my
Ear to supposedly hear an echo
Of the reverberating ocean and
Maybe I heard the faintest whispering

Maybe I was only imagining
As I was listening attentively.

Maybe the cosmos
was listening to me
in the form of a
queen conch seashell that
resembles an ear.

Fifth Avenue is empty of people
Which is strange for New York City as the
Army Corps of Engineers is making
Field Hospitals in Central Park and in

The Javits Center as the city is
Acquisitioning beds from the vacant
Hotels while the nurses and doctors are
Overworked and are catching the virus

No different from doctors and nurses
In Michigan Illinois Florida
And Louisiana while in the rest
Of America the people aren't so

Oppressed though everyone is staying
Home and keeping distance from each other.

Consuming news
Americans risk
infection from
petty reporters
and politicians.

Thinking is so easy to do without
The slightest effort and I don't want to
Stop my cogitation because it's quite
Amusing when I'm balanced and besides

Without a storehouse of thoughts how could I
Converse with friends which is a pleasure I
Couldn't live without but I practice Zen
To let my thoughts come and go by holding

Them gently within the oval I am
Making of my hands sampling in the
Process the tang of emotion attached
To every thought practicing the skill of

Letting go of thought feeling as I do
The dissolution of disturbances.

What my mind does
to weigh me down with
entanglements is a
habit I don't have to
entertain.

I gave my ex-wife all of our photos
Without hesitation but while going
Through the debris of her room looking in
In a box I discovered photos of

A Christmas more than twenty years ago
Of brightly wrapped presents under a tree
Of kittens long since grown and passed away
Of my wife and me without wrinkles and

She is so beautiful and I am young
Again but what's stunning are the happy
Faces of our children Joshua and
Jocelyn innocent and joyous

Before they went to elementary
School and our home was a sanctuary.

The faces of our children
without a hint of
apprehension are
bursting with love.

We are connected electronically
Seeing each other's faces on-line having
Video streaming conferences taking
The communication we need during

Our physical distancing while we are
Advised to wear masks when shopping for food
Because in the intensive care units
Of hospitals across America

People with the virus are struggling
Reducing their focus of awareness
Grasping the next breath feeling as if their
Lungs were filled with glass terrifying the

Nurses and doctors who are caring for
Them so vulnerable to infection.

The fulcrum of
America's effort to
contain the virus is
separation.

The bicycle is heavy with large tires
And riders on racing bikes are passing
Me and frustrating me but there is
The afternoon sun and chilly breezes

And the scenery downtown Stillwater
And a lengthy stretch along the river
Leading to an avenue in the sky
Called the Crossing Bridge taking me into

The Wisconsin countryside where I
Turn about for home while throughout my ride
From the spring-time flooding of the river
And from the wayside ponds I'm noticing

Something new to me that Jason revealed
On our walk — the ticking of chorus frogs

The steep incline of
Myrtle Street at the
end of my ride where
I gasp for breath
is on my mind.

A blustery day yanks on the roots of
Trees agitating and spurring them into
A resurrection of the budding leaves
While I am striving on my bicycle

Leaving the shield of an embankment and
Ascending the extended approach to
The Crossing Bridge in the open air and
I am pedaling vigorously and

Buffeted by the wind at a lofty
Height that only the birds experience
Making me resort to a lighter gear
Straining against the ragged surges of

Wind with labored breath and wearied legs I
Admire the feathery aplomb of birds.

The hill and homes
block the northeast wind
as I ascend Myrtle Street
against the gradient.

I haven't got the gist of using the
Video capacity of the app
So I can hear my sober friends but can't
See them for the online meeting and

Today there are new people from distant
Places whom I haven't met so I use
The quality and emphasis of their
Voices to convey personality

Allowing my imagination to
Form an image of their faces but I
Recognize most of us from many years
Of experience and the message is

Always the same — not to drink today — and
I look forward to seeing the new ones.

Grasping sobriety
can be like climbing
a rope hand over hand —
or like giving a friend
a hand up.

Words are always disputable which is
What I discovered when a friend and I
Started a writer's group in Kyoto with
A master poet named Cid Corman and

Cid brought excellent poetry to read
And he challenged every word that I wrote
And because I hadn't digested life
Enough I gave up poetry for Zen

When years later a poem burst from me
Prompting me to ransack everyday mind
To examine every sensation and
To question every fleeting perception

To seek for ways to dispel delusion
And now I need to learn how to relax.

The mind is a bowl
open to the cosmos
once the clamor
of thinking becomes
quiet.

The lake was reflecting the overcast
Sky in ripples characteristic of
Water so fluidly and even though
It was a gray day in spring I could see

Brightness testifying to the power
Of the sun that despite a covering
Of clouds everything was visible with
Razor clarity with geese among the

Reeds across the far side of the water
Their honking reaching us from a distance
As we were talking about having friends
The difficulty of loneliness and

The weight of broken relationships and
Dog food at a hundred dollars a month.

Your life rotates about
walking with Aries
your poodle two or three
times a day.

The gradient of Myrtle Street rises
Precipitously but it's becoming
Less intimating with each ascent
As it rises in two sections with a

Flatter part in-between and the
First section is only a taste of
Happy difficulty to come when I
Settle on the proper gear and rise from

The seat and stand running on the pedals
Seeing the cracks on the street heart beating
Lungs filling exhaling at the limit
Of capacity determination

Wavering with glimpses up to a bend
Around which I finally see the top.

At the top is
victory
satisfaction
just a little
easier this time.

It's been too cold for the bicycle for
Several days because a northern front has
Descended on Minnesota at the
Very tipping point of spring and so for

Sanity in my isolation I
Am walking for exercise watching the
Snow melting upon the pavement for an
Afternoon that is an oddity of

The temperature being much colder
Above and not so much below as I
Am striding over the Crossing Bridge with
The wind battering my body and face

And forcing me to almost close my eyes
Seeing snow falling sideways in the wind.

A warm snow is
lashing me about
and the river below is
invisible.

They appear again in spring about as
Numerous as the squirrels while keeping their
Distance from people though they aren't afraid
To gaze at us for a moment before

Scampering away and seeing their mode
Of ambulation does make me think of
The kangaroo sharing elongated
Hind legs and powerful haunches designed

For springing jumps which in practice gives them
An odd hopping gait and they also have
The kangaroo's lengthy ears and somewhat
Pointy nose but as they're little creatures

It's easy to overlook their presence
Unless a person is a gardener.

I don't care for
growing flowers
or vegetables so I've
got nothing against
the rabbits.

The lampshade in the corner is glowing
Yellow of a tint less brightly and more
Gentle than the light dispersed onto the
Walls below the shade as the sun rising

In the east is now prominent enough
To pour itself into the living room
From the west window to clarify the
Studio piano the drawing of

The Chinese man and the wooden table
As the back of the steel stop sign across
The street is transformed by the angle of
The sun into a brilliant disk of light

Becoming almost another sun as
Painful to look at as the sun itself.

I can see the
sun touching
the branches of
the lilac bush
on the corner

While I was walking over the lofty
St. Croix Crossing Bridge and seeing such a
Panorama of clouds and the mighty
River glimmering in the sunlight so

Far below me I remembered that
William Wordsworth wrote a sonnet about
A quiet morning view of London from
Westminster Bridge as the ships and domes

And theaters and temples of the calm
Majestic city were glistening in the
Silent and smokeless air as described in
His lines arrayed with rhyming ends and I

Took pleasure in imagining the scene
A vanished cynosure of history.

Walking on the Crossing Bridge
I shared something of the
mighty beating heart
that Wordsworth felt
shorn of ornamentation.

A friend whom I would like to know better
Says that I'm more fluent with poetry
Than in our conversation together
Which is an insightful assessment but

I am aware of the tripwires of our
Differences if I disregarded
Would lead to unpleasant disagreements
Making me defensively circumspect

Contrary to my desire as she's not
Aware of how joyfully present I
Could be given a more harmonious
Mixture of personality — which is

No one's fault — so I've fallen into my
Pattern of being a good listener.

Maybe we have to
make do until
the missing pieces
of our puzzles
come together.

At 4:30 a.m. Kitcat rises
On his haunches striking my bedroom door
Like a drum with his front paws one after
The other insisting I get up and

Occasionally I wait testing his
Determination but eventually
I open up and he and Johnnie burst
In with Johnnie whining to be fed while

Kitcat lunges onto the bed and up
On a chest of drawers next to a marble
Urn holding a dozen peacock feathers
And he sniffs licks and nibbles the frilly

Parts every morning trying my patience
When I ask him what he thinks he's doing.

I pick him up
look into his eyes
toss him onto the bed
and he scrambles
away.

I'm hesitant to write about my phone
Because I'm prideful and am mindful that
If someone reads my poem a hundred
Years from now I could be amusing by

Praising the marvelous technology
Allowing me with a hand-held device
To connect to the Internet and with
Satellites thereby accessing so much

Of humanities' collected knowledge
As a person reading a hundred years
From now could be using technology
So superior that he would snicker

At my quaint fascination as if a
Smartphone were like a horse and a buggy.

Do we really expect
technology to keep
quadrupling power
without incurring
nemesis?

People in America for weeks have
Been keeping a distance from each other
To mitigate the spread of the virus
And the actual numbers of the dead

Are far less than the predictions casting
Doubt on the justifications for the
Strangulation of the economy
With the hardship and insecurity

Imposed on those of precarious means
But we will never know how many would
Have died but for the stay-at-home orders
While the burden of providing food and

Care has fallen on doctors nurses truck
Drivers and the supermarket workers.

The cashier
at the local Walmart
processing payments
for groceries is
essential.

A person gets attached to the first cup
Of coffee and to leaving home at a
Normal time to meet a predictable
Group of people even though everything

Is constantly changing with each precious
Friendship destined to disappear some day
It's so easy to be lulled into a
Sense of permanence by a gradual

Pace of metamorphosis making just
A single deviation from the norm
Noticeable when the emergence of
The worldwide pandemic like an earthquake

Upturning the smallest details of life
Moved beyond our grasping the way things were.

But people are
also stubbornly
persistent and
given to mass
amnesia.

Jason takes bounding steps on the trails of
William O'Brien State Park that he walks
For exercise and because he is an
Ecologist he knows why the oaks and the

White paper birch are growing on one side
Of the hill and the juniper are on
The other explaining as he does to
Me as I'm stretching my stride and pace to

Keep the conversation going about
The way sometimes a hunch will bring him to
A stop in the woods almost as if he's
Called by a consciousness of the landscape

Proceeding carefully stepping slowly
To find a lotus that shouldn't be there.

I discover two days
later my left big toenail
is bruised and black because
my socks were too thick
my boots a little too small.

Things happen without my thinking about
Them like the way my eyes are blinking keeping
Themselves moist or the way my tongue is a
Ballerina acrobatically

Flexing and modulating subtle sounds
And I don't have to make a decision
To sneeze or cough as they ambush me with
Vehemence embarrassing me at such

Awkward moments and if I were in charge
Of beating my heart and breathing my lungs
I wouldn't have the pleasure of my quiet
Selections from which my poetry comes

But it is especially marvelous
How a bruised toenail takes care of itself.

An odd pain persisted
from my left big toenail
and now it's blackened
and getting ready to
fall off.

While I am sitting on my cushion and
Meditating the St. Croix Crossing Bridge
Is in my mind along with the clouds the
Sunshine and the buffeting wind that may

Be blowing on me from behind which makes
My pedaling easy or if I'm facing
A crossing or a head wind then my legs
And lungs are stressed because I like to go

As fast as I can as a test of my
Determination as I am sitting
On my cushion meditating as a
Thought flickers and disappears of what I

Want to do this sunny afternoon and
Then I return to pregnant emptiness.

It's hard to specify
what the nourishment
of emptiness is but
I can write about my
bicycle.

A body has to have a harmony
Of parts to compose a sensible form
Of locomotion and it's curious
To say how the creature came to be with

Its tiny front legs and five fingered paws
Opposed to its enormous haunches and
Elongated rear paws balanced by a
Sinewy long tail as a view of the

Whole including lengthy and upright ears
And pointy face seems a concoction of
Absurdity bereft of dignity
Lopsided hopping lopsided hopping

Slowly moving finically about
The earth stooping over to munch the grass.

Only when the
red kangaroo is
springing into speed
is the music of form
revealed.

In the distance the rain was falling in
Barely visible lines of gray but the
Clouds over us were scattered and when we
Stopped to look at them after so many

Hours of vigorous striding and maybe
Because my pulse was elevated and
I was beyond the point of exhaustion
The clouds appeared to be drifting away

So rapidly as if I'd never seen
Them properly before in a moment
Of appreciation that the sky and
Clouds and sun are always overhead as

A counterbalance to entanglements
Providing light and rain and detachment.

Jason and I were
talking about life on
planets and moons
apart from seasons.

We passed copses of aspen interspersed
With white paper birch as Jason would stoop
Over to notice a flowering plant
That wasn't colorful and didn't look

Like a flower to me while he pointed
To the outlines of the glacial river
Ten thousand years ago recounting a
Massive movement of the water leaving

Gravelly sand of coarse and fine grains with
Flat plains at different elevations
Separated by steep slopes and with the
Deposits of sediment in places

Over a hundred feet but not so much
Where bedrock is nearer to the surface.

Beyond the
memorization
of species is every
unique season
with surprising
discoveries.

Most of yesterday was rainy and the
Water soaked into the earth and we have
Had warmer sunny days before yesterday
And have also had rainy days before

Yesterday but we have not yet had a
Soaking rainy day followed by sunny
Warm days surely precipitating the
Voracious upraising growth of the grass

Before yesterday and today we are
Looking forward to a liberating
Spring as every year has a calendar
Demarcation of the end of winter

But a calendar isn't lively and
We know when spring has finally arrived.

All the previously
bare bushes and branches
of trees in the neighborhood
are sprouting bright
little buds.

From year to year the signs of change are hard
To remember whether this far along
In Minnesota it's normal at the
Ending of April for the air to be

So stubbornly chilly in the morning
That the furnace remains useful and the
Windows are better shut as I'm walking
About the house evaluating my

Life in comparison with others when
On stepping out with the trash I see a
Robin perched on a twig of the apple
Tree and hear the robin singing the song

That robins do in the morning and I
Hear the air is alive with singing birds.

Marvelous birds
remind me the very
air is alive with
energy apart from
evaluations.

To a squirrel my cottonwood with its
Enormous width and height would appear as
A pillar upholding the world as it
Towers over everything else and the

Tiniest twigs at the very top would
Mark the furthermost end of a journey
Into space with the deepest grooves of the
Bark serving as a ready highway for

The gripping clambering eagerness of
The squirrel climbing easily around
And around the circular trunk giving
A different and an awesome vista

With every higher turn of the circuit
With each turn a happy exploration.

To a squirrel a
cottonwood is a house
of many mansions
especially when buds
are reappearing.

If I were a squat individual
With a prodigious weight heaped upon me
With four stubby legs situated well
Apart and forming a rectangular

Mode of ambulation limiting my
Forward striding to little steps little
Steps I suppose my attention would be
Focused mostly on the sensations of

The earth and the doings of the soil and
Plants and worms and insects with perhaps an
Occasional tear with a hungry fox
Or a coyote but every itch would be

Unreachable and the sky and the moon
Would be a dimension beyond knowing.

I wonder whether
cognition mirrors
the lassitudinous
gait of the
tortoise?

How small we are in comparison to
Mountains and oceans and deserts and how
Stridently we assert our importance
As the Pyramids of Giza and the

Pillars of Luxor attest as such pains
Were taken to align the places of
Worship and burial with the passage
Of the burning sun over rocks and sand

Yet even with radio telescopes
Detecting evidence of the **Big Bang**
It seems that we will never escape the
Bounds of our ever-present horizon

In the distance as we are beings quite
Encumbered with an aversion to death.

The earth is round
spinning eastwards
relative to the sun —
the horizon is moving
1000 miles an hour.

In Japan they celebrate the ending
Of April and the beginning of May
As golden week as the penetrating
Cold has departed and the sweltering

Heat has not arrived while cherry trees and
Wisteria are blooming and the air
Is perfectly temperate prompting the
People to gather in the parks spreading

Blankets on the grass under the cherry
Trees for the passing of conversation
While sitting and seeing the precious blue
Light flickering in pink cherry blossoms

As year after year the seasons pivot
With the blooms of cherry evanescence.

On any day
drops of rain
could scatter the
flowering
quickly.

I assumed that the birds were like people
With each bird capable of a medley
Of songs but my walking with Jason is
Dangerous because he exposes my

Misconceptions knowing as he does that
Each type of bird has its own pattern of
Sound recognizable to the others
Of its kind and birders know this because

They've dedicated years to listening
To birds being birds as birders are the
Kind of people who happily do that
Sort of thing noticing the patterns of

Habitation migration markings of
Feathers and the signature mating calls.

Barn swallow — tit-tit-tit-tit
black-crowned night heron — quawlk
black-capped chickadee — fee-bee
black-chinned hummingbird — tchew
blue-gray gnatcatcher — zpeee

In Japan I heard a warbler in spring
Singing from a stand of fir trees and the
Sound was a liquid loveliness that I
Could never have imagined beforehand

And even though the song has passed I do
Remember its effect some thirty years
Ago and I learned that the Japanese
Call the bird the *uguisu* and the

Name is an imitation of its song
The very sound that cast a spell on me
But just reading or reciting the name
Isn't the same as hearing the bird so

Suddenly and unsuspectingly that
Such unearthly beauty is possible.

After the *uguisu*
the walking path became
quiet.

I was aghast when Jason remarked that
The birds are repeating patterns of song
That improvisation isn't their thing
That they aren't like jazz musicians digging

A riff that was a cherished assumption
Of mine because it's disappointing to
Discover without a doubt that I was
Wrong when six books ago I published a

Poem writing emphatically that
The *uguisu* doesn't repeat a
Pattern but because of Jason now I
Know that the *uguisu* in fact does

And I'm grasping for dubious angles
To wriggle out of my exact wording:

Humans listen intently
recreating bird song
into syllables trying
to grasp the ethereal
with a net.

Repetition with variety is
A spice of life as I wonder whether
A robin is capable of singing
Exactly the same song and whether my

Handwriting traces a similar or
A copy of my signature as each
Of my sonnets produces fourteen ten
Syllable lines but sometimes I'm writing

About Jason and other times about
Red Kangaroos — and the earth and moon and
Sun generate predictable patterns
But the timing varies through the years as

Tulips come before cherry and lilac
Blossoms but they are all late this season.

The sky is glorious
red and yellow tulips
are glowing in the
sunrise but it's
as cold as March.

I'm seeing again the leaves coming out
As the tulips are glowing in the light
As little pinkish buds are appearing
On both of my apple trees which I know

From experience will produce lovely
White blossoms with the sweetest scent that I
Have to be close to enjoy which informs
Me that the bumblebees must have better

Noses than I do otherwise why would
The apple tree bother with creating
Perfume so I'm wondering what are the
Lilac bushes doing on the corner

Of my property as I do not see
A hint of their laggardly flowering.

They also produce
the sweetest perfume
with the variety
of three shades
of purple.

With the pandemic continuing we
Sober alcoholics have taken to
Meeting in Pioneer Park sitting well
Apart from each other in the folding

Chairs that each of us brings partaking of
The principles we practice and swapping
Stories with an elevated view of
The valley and the sun-speckled river

Stretching in the distance before us but
What I enjoyed was the brightest spring sky
Scattered with the clouds when I discovered
How lovely it is to lose myself in

The ethereal sight of a single
Cloud drifting and transforming in the wind.

Wisps and wings
curling and stretching
glowing in the light
gray underneath
constantly changing.

I have an idea to assist the
Beleaguered national government in
Our befuddlement and perplexity
Dealing with the Coronavirus and

With the accumulating national
Debt — why don't we mint about a thousand
Trillion dollar coins approximately
The size of Frisbees that could be made of

One hundred percent sterling silver with
The United States Seal on one side and
The image of President Donald Trump
On the other paying for everything

Which could lead to a fascinating game
Of spinning the magic coin through the air.

Whoever caught
a waffling disc
could become an instant
phenomenon —
a *trillionaire*.

After months of seeing the bare branches
They aren't noticeable anymore as
They're just a part of a scenery that
Isn't changing and then the air becomes

Temperate on some days but returns to
Cooler temperatures as the grass is
Green again after rainy days though the
Grass is growing slowly because the air

Remains stubbornly chilly but then on
An afternoon my eyes are opened to
The presence of the leaves again so bright
In the sunshine and everything seems young

Again in the blue light of spring lifting
The glowing clouds transforming in the sky.

Suddenly the leaves
are here swaying
and sighing in the
breezes like friends
returning.

I'm grateful for the gardeners of
Stillwater when I'm driving about town
Because when I'm rushing to do a chore
Their efforts lighten my day with just a

Glance aside on Everett Street to a
Terrace of soil upraising yellow and
Red tulips appearing as splashes of
Happiness that I didn't have to earn

Contemplating as I do the cups of
Tulips radiating the harmony
Of sun and rain and warmth returning for
Another season of growth apart from

Whatever duty is propelling me
I remember there is joy in living.

The tulips are
the sunlight
visible in
exquisite
form.

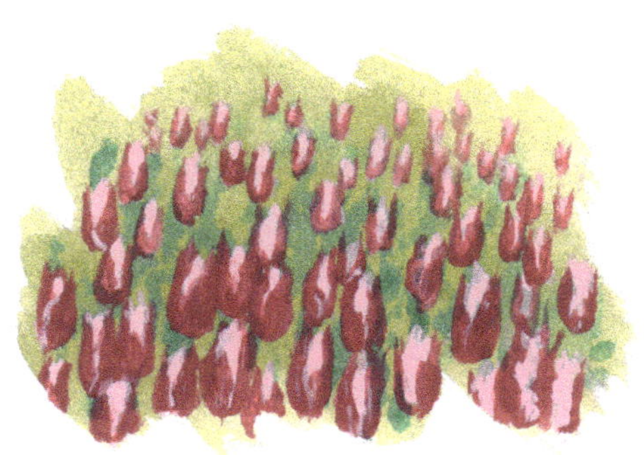

Round bootlaces were like thorns sticking in
My toes as nothing so dissipates my
Dignity as having to keep bending
Over to retie the damn bootlaces

But then Jason showed me how to double
Knot the laces — go over and under
And then make the rabbit ears and then tie
The rabbit ears as I would normally

But then decisively I should take the
Laces and the rabbit ears together
And tie them exactly as I had tied
The rabbit ears initially thusly

I have double knots on both of my boots
And could walk unhindered to Timbuktu.

It's a revelation
to discover how
much ignorance
I've been putting
up with.

A crab is a creature that looks crusty
And to be crabby is to be a drag
So why do we say that the lovely trees
Blooming along with cherry and apple

Trees but generating a deeper more
Luscious one might even say opulent
Darkly pink bordering on red flower
Why do say they are crabapple trees

Because when driving in Stillwater and
Seeing again after the bareness of
Winter the crabapple blooms unfolding
Little by little to their flowering

I feel the weight of winter dissolve with
A taste of crabapple liberation.

I'm not a bee
I don't pollinate
but winter is weighty
year after year and
blooms are liberating.

The oaks are budding after the aspen
And white paper birch with their buds being
About the size of a mouse's ear as
Jason explained while the cells are now as

Numerous as when fully grown meaning
The size of each cell will expand until
The form of the oak leaf is manifest
Signifying that the observations

Of ecologists are bringing to light
The intricacies and energies of
Life indicating that a portion of
Humanity sees beyond the trappings of

Money property and prestige and yet
Who knows what direction we are heading?

Perhaps our wisdom is
like the budding oak leaf
about the size of a
mouse's ear.

I remember a summer afternoon
When my dad gave me a bucket and a
Dandelion picker as he urged me
To expend my energy ridding the

Lawn of weeds for the colossal sum of
Five dollars which I did and even now
My mom who is over eighty years old
Is using the same picker to rid the

Lawn of weeds while now I know what the poor
Have always known that dandelions can be
Eaten and maybe I'm lazy but I've
Learned to appreciate the yellow bloom

Along with the purple Creeping Charlie
And I'm using my energy elsewise.

Perhaps my neighbors
are annoyed with me
for indulging weeds
and maybe I've found
a new way to be smug.

I haven't turned on the printing press for
Six years and I sold it about a year
And a half ago to a printer who will
Use it for parts as it's not worth very

Much and weighs over nine hundred pounds which
Maybe is why he's taken so long to
Come get it even though he said he would
So to me the obsolete machine became

A symbol of inertia sitting there
Uselessly collecting dust but about
Twenty years ago I proudly learned the
Tricks of the trade while also keeping my

Hands clean and I really took pleasure in
Listening to mechanical music.

Two big guys
with barely enough
smarts muscle
and leverage
took it away.

I was running the press when my Dad walked
Into the printing room from the garage
Just after he learned that his long-time friend
And business partner had died of pneumonia

Struggling for breath and I saw a shocked
And frightened expression on my Dad's face
Because Guy Johnson had a confidence
And common sense wisdom about him that

Balanced my Dad's more frenetic nature
And provided my Dad with a sense that
Everything was going to become OK
And I knew that on that day my Dad

Had lost an irreplaceable pillar of strength
And I saw my Dad's defenses were shattered.

On that day
my Dad's face
momentarily
expressed what
his words couldn't.

Stillwater is a hilly town and when
I leave home to do my circuit over
The Crossing Bridge into the countryside
And back again on my bicycle I

Start from the north hill to the downtown of
Stillwater but from then on I'm climbing
Until the furthermost limit of my
Ride and at the section over the bridge

High above the valley I encounter
The buffeting of a side or of a
Head wind impeding my pedaling but
When the wind is pushing me I move in

Silence absorbing the warmth of the sun
And exulting in the effortless speed.

On any given day
at some point on my
circular route the wind
challenges and
exhilarates me.

The understanding of political
Controversy is like the handling
Of the Russian dolls that hide smaller dolls
Within them with the largest doll being

The media sport of making victims
And villains with the frolic of public
Accusation that somehow overlooks
The motives of the accuser but the

Secrets of the intricacies and the
Histories of the issues involving
The interests of the politicos are
Well concealed within the receding dolls

While the hardworking citizen isn't
Aware of the thrust of malevolence.

From an idealistic
point of view the
innermost doll
represents only
questions.

I've not been going through the trouble of
Lifting the garage door and driving the
Car inside anymore as the weather
Is warmer now and the apple blossoms

Are in bloom by my driveway looking in
A glance very much like popcorn and on
The bicycle yesterday I could smell
The perfume of the flowering trees on

The avenues of Stillwater and I'd
Have to be dead not to appreciate
The explosion of white and pink blossoms
In passing while the leaves are almost grown

In contrast to the bareness of branches
Weeks ago and the leaves are so brilliant.

Even with a gray sky
with rain drops falling
this morning spring colors
are bursting with joyous
energy.

On the one hand nature appears lovely
In the shape of apple blossoms and on
The other aggressive as when buckthorn
Spreads across the country by way of the

Robins eating the buckthorn berries and
Pooping the buckthorn seeds about or the
Way sparrows were brought from England to eat
The detestable larvae infecting

The trees in the parks of New York City
With the sparrows spreading across the land
Or the way the Burmese Python is so
Dominant in the everglade grasses

Of Florida because people kept the
Pythons as pets yet somehow they got loose.

People played a part
in the invasiveness
of species yet people
are also invasively
natural.

My driving experience in Japan
Was different on a motorcycle
And a scooter as I was vulnerable
On the frenetic streets of Kyoto to

The trucks and buses and taxis as the
Japanese are accustomed to beeping
Their horns without the animosity
We Americans do as they will beep

Merely to let a driver know that they
Are present and I found myself getting
Upset as if I were quite unjustly
Being scolded and in an instant I

Became angry regardless of daily
Meditation as habit is ingrained.

People emote
differently from
place to place.

If I wrote my own obituary
Today as a service to the people
I would point out that you shouldn't pronounce
Hippopotamus slowly because if

You did others would think you were depressed
Or they may suspect you were trying to
Be funny because sincerity
Of purpose mandates that the syllables

Come out in pell-mell fashion with little
Inflection as the attention of the
Listeners should go to the creature and
Not the word — and as a further service

To humanity I would ask readers
When did you last say hippopotamus?

If a person isn't
saying hippopotamus
once in a while
it's a sign of a
cloistered life.

When moving the snow off the driveway of
My responsibility I yearn for
The overlapping appearance of the
Tulips apple trees and lilacs blooming

In a crescendo of renewing growth
In Stillwater rising into flower
With apple blossoms by my driveway
With Creeping Charlie and dandelions

Underneath with the various perfumes
Mingling about the air which must be a
Bumblebee's heaven but then after a
Day of persisting rain I see on the

Pavement and the grass under both of my
Apple trees what seems to be confetti.

The blooming and
dispersion varies from
flower tree and bush
and the parade lasts
more than a month.

I am a colossus striding about
The house with a banished ex-wife with things
Being exactly where I left them and
I am a beneficent captain with

Johnnie scampering underfoot and with
Kitcat lying upon me when I am
Sequestered on the couch deciding when
To feed them invested with the power

To turn the doorknobs and to open the
Necessary containers only this
Morning Kitcat finagled the doorknob
And suddenly they burst into the room

Jumping onto the bed rousing me from
Quietude and demanding to be fed.

Kitcat is
cleverly
dangerous
and needs to
be watched.

I am a colossus striding about
The house with a banished ex-wife with things
Being exactly where I left them and
I am a beneficent captain with

Johnnie scampering underfoot and with
Kitcat lying upon me when I am
Sequestered on the couch deciding when
To feed them invested with the power

To turn the doorknobs and to open the
Necessary containers only this
Morning Kitcat finagled the doorknob
And suddenly they burst into the room

Jumping onto the bed rousing me from
Quietude and demanding to be fed.

Kitcat is
cleverly
dangerous
and needs to
be watched.

Suddenly a flit in the air alerts
Me as I am leaving the store that the
Swallows of Walmart have retuned again
And I don't know why a strip mall attracts

Them and don't know how far they've traveled
Or whether these are the same birds of last
Year and I wonder whether their turning
Cutting and fleeting in the air as if

They were blades is joyful for them but I'm
Grateful for the openness of the sky
Even with the horizon of big box
Stores any moment as quick as lightning

As long as I am clear-headed and poised
That I may see something marvelous.

Riding my bicycle
at a certain spot along
the river I am assailed
about my ears mouth and eyes
by gnats.

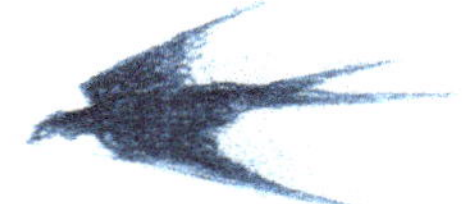

Letters are tricky and capable of
Invisibility as when I typed
"Raise" when intending to type "rise" which went
Unnoticed for several days until an

Instant of recognition made me hit
Myself in the forehead with a fist as
Overlooking the obvious is what
I do and making marks upon a page

Assuming someone else will spend the time
In reading them is a presumption I
May not earn and composing poems is
Like being a trapeze artist swinging

On a rope preparing to launch myself
Into the air and hoping to be caught.

I love the spontaneity
and moment of
assertion within
communication.

Even with the east wind against me as
I'm pedaling over the Crossing Bridge
Seeing the little ripples below me
Of the wide expanse of the river I

Can imagine I'm conquering the
River and mastering the elements
Whether the day is cloudy or sunny
As hard as the wind may blow I have the

Stamina and proper gears to make it
Across absorbing the panorama
Into my being but the life-giving
Movement of water is continuous

Southwards along a valley of the earth
And I can chuckle at my presumption.

The river passes through
every living being
becomes an ocean
drifting clouds and a
creek in the woods.

When the leaves are fully grown then most of
The apples blossoms are upon the grass
And spring rain is saturating the soil
And the grass is growing voraciously

And does need to be mowed regularly
Otherwise the mower will become clogged
Making me yank on the cord to start it
Again which I'd rather not do as it

Is getting harder to start but I am
Learning to appreciate mowing the
Grass once in a week and leveling the
Creeping Charlie and the dandelions

But this year I've found I'm a little sad
When its time to mow the apple blossoms.

The annual parade
of blossoms in spring
that I anticipate
in winter is
disintegrating.

I don't get close enough to observe them
But I heard them before the leaves came out
Making a chorus of background music
Sounding continuously in the spring

And I hardly noticed until Jason
Told me what they were the little creatures
With bug eyes and squishy bodies who puff
Themselves to expel the air and announce

Their presence and aesthetically they
Are just odd and ugly enough to be
Ludicrously pleasing jumping as they
Do with springy legs and snatching insects

On the fly with their adroitness of tongues
As our children learn in their early years.

I heard the peepers
chorus and wood frogs
for many years
without awareness.

They traipse about the town in families
Strolling on the grass near the ponds and lakes
With the parents leading and the fuzzy
Newborns following in a line making

A caravan and they aren't afraid to
Cross a road and bring the traffic to a
Halt as they exhibit a confident
Dignity that projects a measure of

Distance between them and others because
The parents are irascible and will
Rush and hiss at intruders but as they
Walk they wobble because of their bulging

Bodies and ridiculously long necks
Culminating into pinched little heads.

They are aerodynamic
as the geese form themselves
into lines like arrows
slipping through the air
going distances.

On the corner of my property next
To a fire hydrant and under the
Cottonwood where the city snowplows are
Misjudging the distance and tearing up

The grass for year after year there are my
Lilac bushes that I look forward to
As a gage of season recalling them
In the snow-bourn depth of February

Because the lilac blossoms are the last
Celebration of spring and the gateway
Into summer marking when the roots of
The grass and the bushes and the trees are

Busy drinking water and minerals
And the leaves are absorbing the sunlight.

My ex-wife planted the
lilacs and they have only
one scent but it's pleasing
they come in three shades
of purple.

The pandemic didn't interrupt the
Accusatory words of politics
But only served to deepen divisions
Of America along party lines

As patriotism separated
Into warring factions a while ago
And presently the arguments concern
Who is to blame for which delinquency

As the nation is reopening for
Business by various degrees in each
Of the fifty states as everyone is
Encouraged to wear a mask in public

And to maintain six feet of distance from
Each other as contagion continues.

Public discourse is
at such a pitch of
acrimony it's hard
to guess what could
unify the nation.

There is a lawyer named Jim
Who managed the FBI
He lied to Congress
And lied on TV
And thinks he's a marvelous guy.

There is a lawyer named Bill
Who directs the DOJ
He's smart as a fox
And follows the law
And Jim is finally going to pay.

America is
celebrating
Memorial Day
for the nation's
soldiers killed
in battle as the
roots of summer
are beginning to
drink water
and minerals.

— *Tekkan*